>>Drive. Ride. Fly.

JOHN DEERE

✤ ROD BEEMER ✤
With Tracy Nelson Maurer

MOTORBOOKS

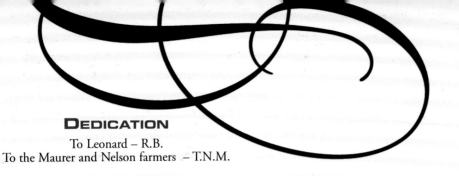

DEDICATION

To Leonard – R.B.
To the Maurer and Nelson farmers – T.N.M.

On the front cover: This 1956 Model 70 Standard Diesel is equipped with a PTO, three-point hitch, adjustable wide front axle, and a V-4 gasoline-starting engine.

On the frontispiece: 1956 Model 70 Standard Diesel

On the title page: A very nice 1936 Model A on wide-rim, round-spoke F&H rear wheels. The owner traded two Model MT tractors for this completely restored Model A.

Table of contents page: A Model MT weighs in at about 2,600 pounds, stands 56 inches high at the radiator, and is 110 inches long. Sure, it isn't a big tractor, but it looks like a toy next to a 27,000-bushel grain bin.

On the back cover: A very nice 1936 Model A on wide-rim, round-spoke F&H rear wheels. The owner traded two Model MT tractors for this completely restored Model A.

Editor: Heather Oakley

Designer: Ryan Schmidt of Koechel Peterson and Associates, Inc., Minneapolis, MN

Printed in China

ACKNOWLEDGMENTS

A grateful thanks go to the following collectors and restorers: Mel Kopf; Kenny Read; Justin Read; Charles Dugan; Albert Jansen; Bob Roblin; Jake Delaney; Clifford Smith; Lester, Kenny, and Harland Layher; Duaine and Orville Filsinger; John Nikodym; LeRay Koons; Ron Jungmeyer; Mrs. Kenneth Peterman; Dan Peterman; Don Nolde; Earl and Harold Hartzog; Leon and Theresa Beedy; Mark Strasser; Leo Zeigler; Andy and Karen Anderson; and Larry Shetter.

Thanks also to Mike Mack, retired director, Product Engineering Center at Deere & Company; and Bill Bulow, retired, Deere & Company Waterloo Foundry.
These dedicated people help keep the history alive.
—R.B.

Thank you to Harlan and Donna Maurer, Jerry Maurer, Kendall and Lois Nelson, and mostly to Mike Maurer for answering every pesky question.
— T.N.M.

John Deere equipment is still hard at work. Drive by almost any residential or commercial construction site, and chances are John Deere equipment is on the job. Travel through rural America, it's a good bet that green and yellow John Deere tractors and equipment will be visible in the fields and farmyards.

CONTENTS

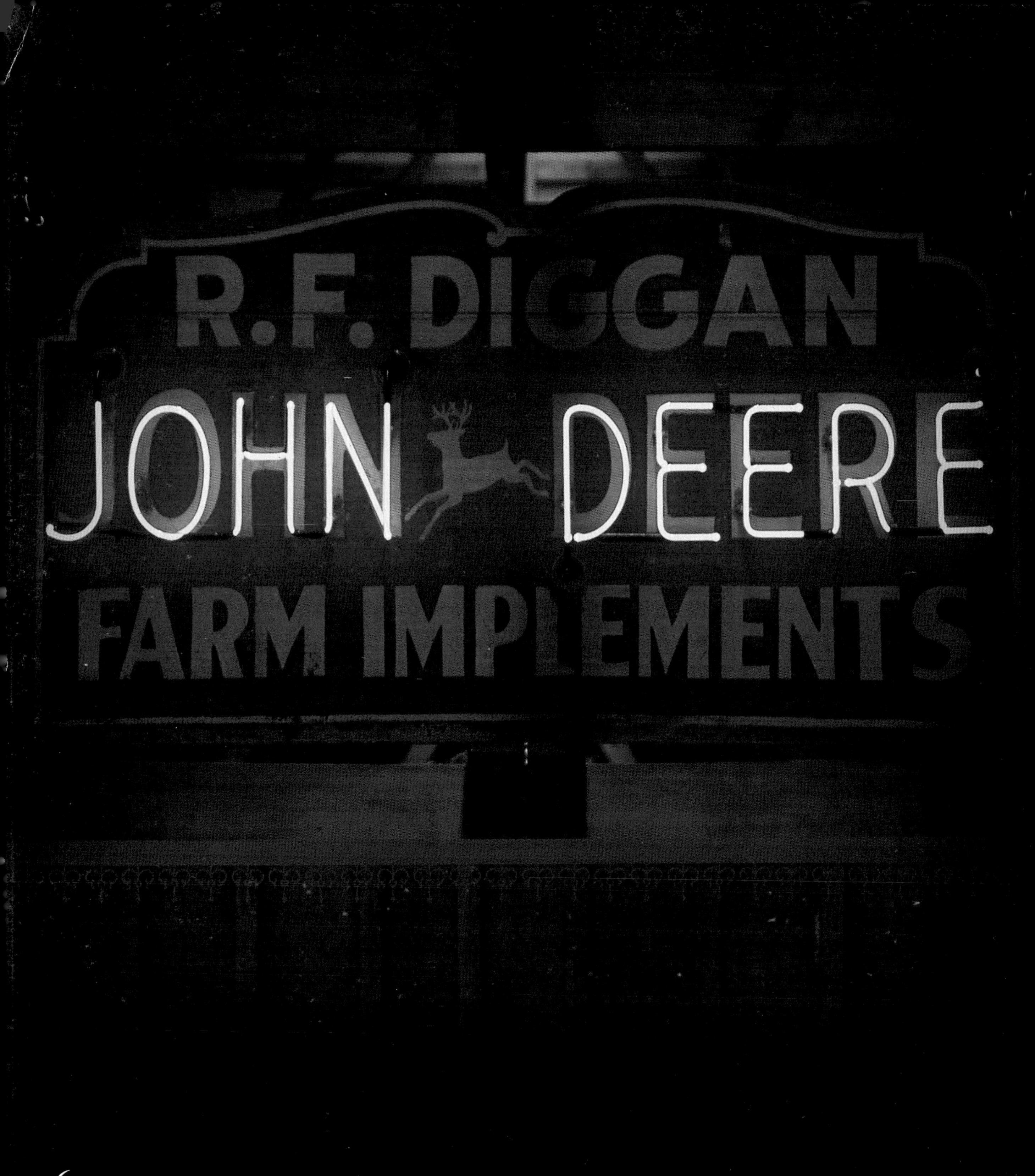
R.F. DIGGAN
JOHN DEERE
FARM IMPLEMENTS

INTRODUCTION

BEFORE YOU DIG INTO THIS BOOK

This book focuses on John Deere two-cylinder tractors and some modern John Deere information.

• You might veer into technical territory on a page or two, but you're not reading a technical manual. Check the glossary for terms you don't know.

• Tractor descriptions may mention production numbers. Sometimes sources for the numbers don't agree. Maybe the actual number of tractors produced for any one model was more; maybe it was less. That's when this book uses approximate numbers.

• If you were born in September 1995, would your parents have called you a 1996 model? Deere & Company would have! Like automobiles, new model John Deere two-cylinder tractors arrived in the fall of each year but Deere & Company used the next calendar year as the model year. This book uses model years, unless noted otherwise.

Look closely at the green and gold on these pages and you'll see countless hours of hard work and pride shining through. You don't have to live or work on a farm to appreciate John Deere's special place in history.

Ready for a serious load of John Deere details? Crank that flywheel and go!

PLOWING INTO THE 20TH CENTURY

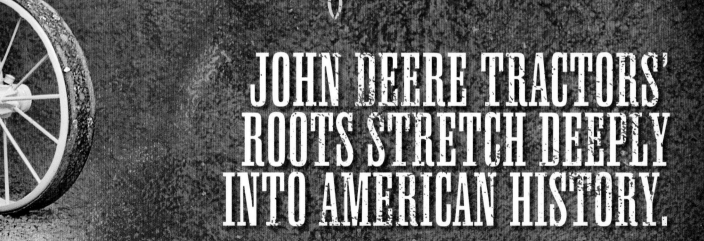

JOHN DEERE TRACTORS' ROOTS STRETCH DEEPLY INTO AMERICAN HISTORY.

From the Waterloo Boy to the 30 Series models, Deere & Company's machines have helped put food on tables, construct roadways, and shape building sites for generations around the world. All of today's ultra-modern, high-tech John Deere tractors trace their ancestry directly back to the two-cylinder tractors.

But before any John Deere tractors putt-putted down the fields, Deere & Company focused on plows—horse-drawn plows.

JOHN DEERE STARTS JOHN DEERE

In the 1800s, agriculture mainly used human and animal muscle. Farmers depended on horse-drawn plows, handmade heavy cast-iron equipment. So it made sense to John Deere to learn the blacksmith trade. Unfortunately, farmers in Vermont weren't buying many new plows then due to a sour economy.

John Deere heard exciting stories about rich, fertile soil and open opportunity on the western frontier. All the while, his debt mounted. In 1836, he packed his tools and traveled west.

Within the year, Deere set up a forge in Grand Detour, Illinois. He built a decent trade by shoeing horses and oxen, fixing cast-iron plows, and making tools for the pioneers.

Local customers complained that the rich Illinois soil stuck to their plows, forcing them to stop every few paces to clear clumps away. The sandy soil back East never gave them that kind of trouble.

John Deere invented a solution using polished steel from an old saw blade. His curved "self-scouring" steel plow kept the farmers from leaving the Midwest. They stayed and planted the roots of America's breadbasket.

SELF-SCOURING PLOW

John Deere tested "marketing" almost 100 years before Corporate America did. Deere first listened to what customers wanted. Then he tested a solution, such as his clever "self-scouring" polished steel plow. Unlike other blacksmiths, Deere built a supply of plows *before* he received any orders, and brought the plows to the farming areas. Farmers could buy them—and use them—that day.

The Nation's Second-Oldest Manufacturer

Although John Deere worked with different partners over the years and changed the business name a few times, Deere's business is likely the second-oldest continuously operating manufacturing firm in the United States.

MERGER MANIA

Congress passed the Sherman Anti-Trust Act in 1890 to clamp down on monopolies, so the empire builders created legal holding companies instead. Foreign money also helped launch round after round of buyouts, mergers, and takeovers. The corporate boardroom motto was "get bigger or get out."

Long before he died in 1886, John Deere had begun handing the business over to his son Charles. Charles favored a merger for the company.

Several investor groups targeted Deere & Company at different times in those early days. They hoped to form a plow trust, or mega implement-manufacturing group, by buying Deere & Company and blending it with other major implement companies. All the deals fell through.

WELCOME TO THE USA

The United States saw its biggest decade for legal immigration between 1901 and 1910 when 8,795,386 people arrived here.
These new Americans wanted to own land—an impossible dream in their native countries. Many became John Deere tractor owners.

The Waterloo Boy Model R "One Man Tractor" was introduced in 1913. The Model N replaced it in 1918.

THE TRACTION CONTRAPTION

In 1892, the first successful (well, sort-of successful) kerosene/gasoline-powered tractors chugged into the picture. These landmark developments in agricultural history didn't stir up much notice—at first, anyway.

Deere & Company stayed focused on the plow business. The firm also made cultivators, corn and cotton planters, and other implements—but not newfangled tractors. The years of merger mania had left fewer competitors to handle the growing demand from Western pioneers. Deere & Company profited.

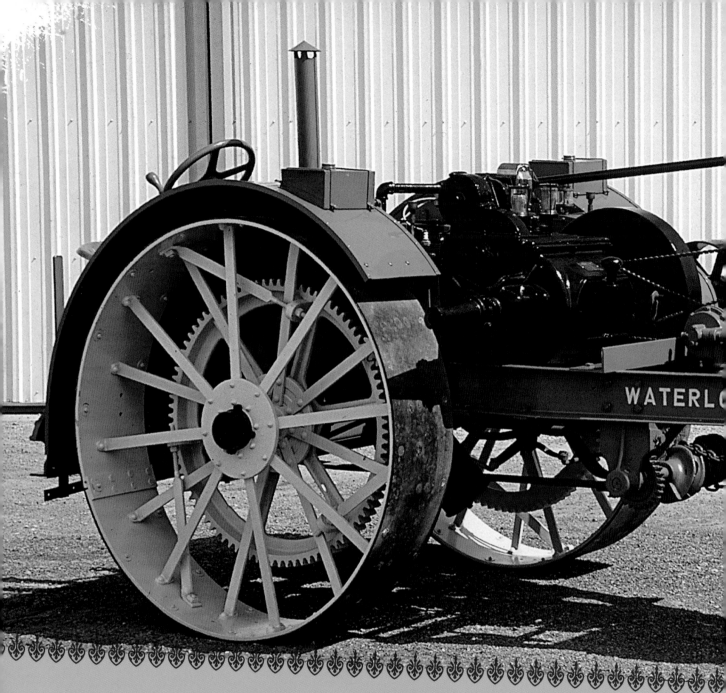

Deere & Company ranked as a small but respected player in the farm implement industry when Charles Deere died in 1907. The board of directors elected William Butterworth as company president. Butterworth saw a tough road ahead for the company, but he kept a steady course. Unemployment climbed, banks failed, and food prices rose dramatically. Fortunately, the "Panic of 1907" didn't last long, and Deere & Company weathered the storm.

KEROSENE

TRACTOR

GO GREEN!

Green and yellow apparently made its debut in 1905 in a Deere & Webber catalog for a Deere plow. Nobody knows why the colors were used, but the combination has stayed through the years.

KEROSENE

BATTLING THE GIANTS

Butterworth faced a business world filled with giant U.S. corporations. In farm machinery, International Harvester Company (IHC) towered over the industry. IHC placed fourth in size among all U.S. corporations in 1909. Only U.S. Steel, Standard Oil, and the American Tobacco Company listed more assets. IHC controlled about 90 percent of the grain binder production and 80 percent of the mower production in the United States.

Then the tractor frenzy hit. Of course, IHC was in the middle of it. Smaller farm implement companies like Deere & Company had to grow to survive. The company tried mergers. The managers even considered a deal with IHC. In the end, they couldn't agree.

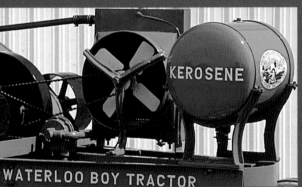

WATERLOO BOY TRACTOR

SOLO BUSINESS

Today, Deere & Company remains the only full-line U.S. agricultural implement and equipment-manufacturing corporation that hasn't been merged or sold. That's impressive now. But for Deere & Company in the early twentieth century, it was troublesome.

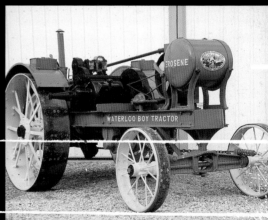

BUILDING THE LINE

JOINING THE GIANTS DIDN'T WORK. BEATING THEM WASN'T GOING TO BE EASY, EITHER.

DEERE & COMPANY LEADERS GEARED UP FOR BATTLE. THEY DECIDED TO MAKE DEERE & COMPANY A FULL-LINE FIRM BY BUYING UP THE NECESSARY MANUFACTURERS.

WHAT IF...?

If Deere & Company had remained a short-line manufacturer—making mainly plows and tillage implements—and if it survived, history suggests that no John Deere tractors would have ever been built. Only full-line companies were successful in the tractor-manufacturing arena.

BIGGER BY TEN BY 1911

In 1910 and 1911, Deere & Company bought ten companies to create a full-line firm. The shopping spree included:

- DAIN MANUFACTURING COMPANY
- MOLINE WAGON COMPANY
- VAN BRUNT MANUFACTURING COMPANY
- UNION MALLEABLE IRON COMPANY
- SYRACUSE CHILLED PLOW COMPANY
- DEERE & MANSUR COMPANY
- KEMP & BURPEE MANUFACTURING COMPANY
- RELIANCE BUGGY COMPANY
- DAVENPORT WAGON COMPANY

Deere & Company managers tried to ignore tractors. The wake-up call came with World War I in 1914.

President Woodrow Wilson boosted the 200,000-man army to nearly five million. As farmers joined the war effort overseas, they left their wives and children to manage the farms. The U.S. government also needed more food from the farms to send to the hungry troops and to ease England's food shortages. The demand for wheat skyrocketed. Tractors answered the call.

By 1917, U.S. production doubled to 62,742 tractors, and doubled again in 1918 to 132,000 vehicles.

STOP THAT TRACTOR!

WATERLOO WHO?

Deere & Company had resisted tractors for years. Ironically, when Deere & Company bought the Waterloo Gasoline Engine Company in 1918, history would forever connect Deere & Company with the original tractor story.

In 1892, John Froelich replaced the steam powerplant on his threshing machine with a gasoline engine and invented the first tractor. The next year he and a few partners organized the Waterloo Gasoline Traction Engine Company in Waterloo, Iowa. Only four of Froelich's tractors rolled out the door. Froelich left the company in 1895.

Renamed as the Waterloo Gasoline Engine Company, the business focused on stationary gasoline-kerosene engines, cream separators, milking machines, and manure spreaders. It pushed tractors aside.

Then in 1911 the company hired inventor A. B. Parkhurst to revive its tractor research. The firm also acquired his three tractor designs. A slight change to his two-cylinder engine helped develop a new, more powerful tractor: the Waterloo Boy Model R, the granddaddy of the John Deere two-cylinder legacy.

DEERE & COMPANY'S $2.35 MILLION TRACTOR

When World War I ended in 1918, about 200 manufacturers were competing for the nation's tractor business. In March 1918, Deere & Company finally joined the tractor frenzy by purchasing the Waterloo Gasoline Engine Company for $2.35 million. The deal gave Deere & Company a modern production facility, a foundry, and the two-cylinder Waterloo Boy tractor.

The Waterloo Boy Model R sold for $985 and the Model N for $1,150.

OVERTIME OVER THERE

Not all Waterloo Boys stayed in the U.S. Harry Ferguson's Belfast, Ireland, auto dealership sold Waterloo Boy tractors under the name Overtime. The Waterloo Gasoline Engine Company manufactured the Waterloo Boys to burn kerosene, but the U.K. Overtime used paraffin—the British versionof kerosene.

TESTING POWER

In 1920, a Waterloo Boy Model N became one of the first tractors tested at the newly established Nebraska Tractor Test Laboratory in Lincoln.

The Nebraska Tractor Test Laboratory resulted from a 1919 Nebraska law designed to check manufacturers' advertised claims of tractor performance. Today, the world-renowned test facility on the University of Nebraska campus is unique in the United States. It continues to measure tractor performance today as it has done for many John Deere tractor models over the years.

The main tests focus on tractor power—especially *horsepower*.

In the late 1700s, James Watt wanted a standard measurement for his steam engines' power. Watt studied ponies working in coal mines. He estimated a pony could lift 550 pounds of coal at a rate of one foot per second or 33,000 pounds to a one-foot height in one minute. He called this unit of power "horsepower"—the same standard used today.

A tractor engine's highest horsepower rating, called the *indicated horsepower*, comes from its cylinder pressure. But not all of the indicated power makes it to the implement attached to the power take-off unit, or PTO. Engine friction, sticky transmissions, axles and tires, and other attachments drag power from the engine.

On tractors that drive the PTO directly from the engine and not through the transmission, the *PTO horsepower* equals the indicated horsepower minus the engine friction. The actual horsepower delivered from the engine to the shaft is also called *brake horsepower*.

Effective horsepower or *drawbar horsepower* reflects the final horsepower sent to the drawbar to pull an implement. Drawbar horsepower is always less than the indicated horsepower, sometimes reduced by 25 percent or more on antique tractors.

Waterloo Boy Model R and Model N

Introduced in 1913, the Waterloo Boy Model R changed about twelve times until it arrived at the Model N. The John Deere Model D replaced the Waterloo Boy in 1924.

THE MECHANICAL ANIMAL

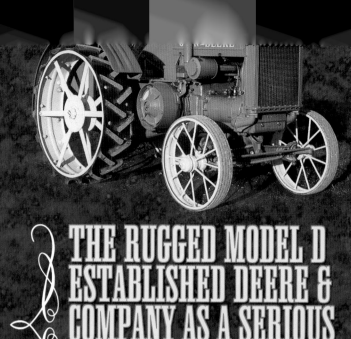

After its big purchase, Deere & Company discovered the Waterloo plant's R&D team was secretly experimenting with a new tractor to replace the aging Waterloo Boy. Deere & Company called it the John Deere Model D.

Despite poor tractor sales and a dismal postwar economy, Deere & Company introduced the hard-working, no-nonsense Model D in 1923. Congress created the Agricultural Credits Act that year to fund farm cooperatives. Farmers could easily borrow money for machinery to replace their horses, mules, and oxen.

The unstyled, or bare-bones, version of the John Deere Model D pitched and rolled but offered durability. One farmer said, "If you can find a one-owner John Deere D, buy it 'cause there ain't no single man that can wear one out."

The rugged Model D established Deere & Company as a serious contender in the tractor business. The mechanical animal underwent numerous upgrades through its stellar 30-year run and earned several nicknames along the way, such as Nickel-Hole Flywheels, Ladder-Siders, Corn Borer Specials, and Streeters.

THE RUGGED MODEL D ESTABLISHED DEERE & COMPANY AS A SERIOUS CONTENDER IN THE TRACTOR BUSINESS.

The belt pulley is on the left side of the Waterloo Boy, located on the outboard side of the flywheel.

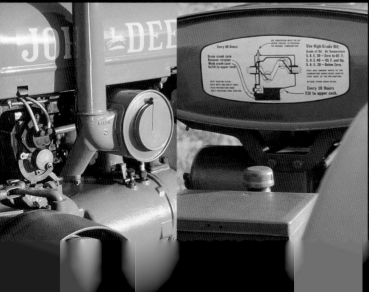

Above: From 1927 on, the Model D engine's 501 cubic-inch displacement was the largest of any two-cylinder John Deere tractor.

Model Ds used a spoked flywheel until December 1925. This 1924 Model D 26-inch Spoker still runs like a champ.

This 1924 Model D uses many same parts as the Waterloo Boy did.

Farmers were just learning about mechanical power and its necessary maintenance in the 1920s. With the decal on the tank, as on this early Model D, the operator had many hours to think about the important instructions.

LISTEN FOR THE JOHNNY POPPERS

JOHN DEERE

Ask any farmer, especially a grandpa, and he'll quickly recall the sound of a two-cylinder John Deere tractor and maybe a story, too.

"Pa-putt..Pa-putt. What a sound! Our neighbor tried to out-sing the racket. You could hear him yodeling from the next field over—that was three quarters of a mile away."

The throaty, metallic exhaust tune rumbled from every two-lunger John Deere tractor. From the Model D in 1924 to the last series in 1960, they all earned the Johnny Popper, Putt-Putt Johnny, or Poppin' Johnny nickname. (The two-cylinder, two-cycle General Motors diesel engine lost the distinctive sound in the 1959/60 Model 435. It's not called a Johnny Popper.)

What made the Johnny Popper pop? Inside each cylinder, one piston pumped through its four-stroke rhythm and fired off the fuel at a slightly different time than the other piston. Then the engine coasted briefly until it fired through the cycle again. The position of the two cylinders, either vertical or opposed, created slightly different tunes.

GENERAL PURPOSE TRACTORS

Row-crop farmers wanted a tractor to pull planters and cultivators. Of the thousands of John Deere cultivators made so far, not one worked properly behind a Waterloo Boy or a Model D tractor.

Worse, one year after the Model D rolled out, huge IHC corporation showcased its new Farmall.

It revolutionized row-crop farming and left Deere & Company in the dust.

The John Deere All-Crop, soon renamed as the Model C, hit production in March 1928. By April, the firm built about 99 Model C tractors. The company recalled at least 53 of these to be rebuilt and renumbered.

This 1927 Model C was mysteriously rebuilt at the factory in March 1928. It's outfitted with a Model 301 three-row planter that farmers never really liked.

Ready For Rubber

Beginning in 1933, rubber tires became available for the Model D as shown on this 1937 version. Optional industrial equipment, including solid rubber tires, were available as early as 1926. Rubber tires became standard equipment in 1941, and the rear-tire size was changed from 28 to 30 inches. World War II rubber shortages briefly brought back steel as standard equipment.

In 1928, Butterworth passed the presidency of Deere & Company to Charles Deere Wiman, John Deere's grandson. The firm put its new Model GPWT (General Purpose Wide-Tread) into production in July 1929. Deere & Company stayed in the row-crop tractor market, but the Farmall pounded John Deere sales.

In October 1929, the U.S. stock market crashed and the Great Depression soon strangled the nation. Tough times and merger mania whittled the full-line farm equipment companies down to IHC,

Deere & Company, Case, Oliver, Allis-Chalmers, Minneapolis-Moline, and Massey-Harris.

It wasn't the first time Deere & Company had a new president and a bad economy. Charles Wiman prepared his firm for the rocky future and told his R&D engineers to build a row-crop winner.

Meanwhile, Deere & Company, now in stiff competition at the top with bigger IHC, kept building the General Purpose tractors—and waited for a breakthrough.

Deere & Company fixed the mechanical errors of the Model C (background) and introduced the new Model GP-General Purpose in August 1928. This is a 1935 Model GP.

Wide Tread certainly meant "wide tread." The 84-inch rear-tread coupled with a tricycle front axle could handle two- or four-row planting and cultivating.

Horse Nonsense

In the 1930s, many small farmers still used horses. Work stopped when the horse tuckered out. A tractor worked all hours and finished as much as five times more work than a horse in the same time. A horse also needed about five acres for its own food. A tractor didn't.

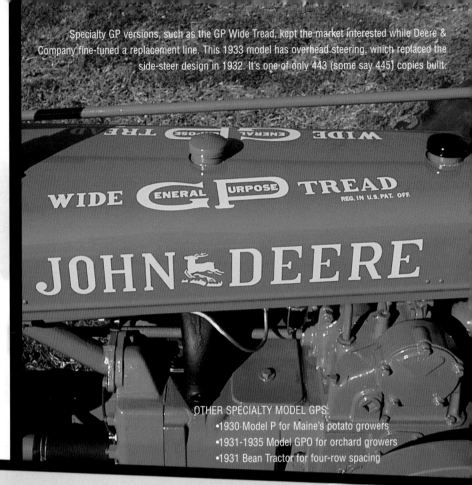

Specialty GP versions, such as the GP Wide Tread, kept the market interested while Deere & Company fine-tuned a replacement line. This 1933 model has overhead steering, which replaced the side-steer design in 1932. It's one of only 443 (some say 445) copies built.

WIDE GENERAL PURPOSE TREAD REG. IN U.S. PAT. OFF.

JOHN DEERE

OTHER SPECIALTY MODEL GPS:
- 1930 Model P for Maine's potato growers
- 1931-1935 Model GPO for orchard growers
- 1931 Bean Tractor for four-row spacing

MUFFLED SALES

The Great Depression muffled sales and forced layoffs, but Deere & Company limped along.

- In 1931, Deere & Company lost $1 million on $27.7 million in sales.
- In 1932, Deere & Company lost $5.7 million on $8.7 million in sales.
- In 1933, Deere & Company lost $4.3 million on $9 million in sales.

Although times were tough, the lights stayed on in the R&D department. In April 1934, the R&D team's general purpose row-crop tractor, the Model A, hit the production line. A smaller brother, the Model B, followed in 1935. They rolled into showrooms in time to cash in on President Franklin D. Roosevelt's Agricultural Adjustment Act, which paid farmers to NOT grow crops.

The government's Farm Security Agency soon followed. This "New Deal" program tried to help smaller farmers. They could take out low-interest government loans.

This 1934 Model A sports dual rear wheels, perhaps for more traction and flotation in sandy or boggy conditions.

Many landowners bought tractors with their government checks. By 1936, tractor sales perked up again.

With the Model A, Farmers could work in 40- or 42-inch rows. An optional hydraulic lift-and-lower system adjusted the implement. Mechanical muscle replaced operator muscle. Improved driver visibility, handling, and comfort sold more Model As and Model Bs than any other John Deere two-cylinder tractors.

Deere & Company built 300,000 copies before it took the Model A out of production in 1952. Over 306,000 Model Bs sold between 1935 and 1952.

Bigger than a Model A or Model B, the powerful Model G added a three-plow workhorse to the Deere & Company lineup in 1937. Production variations ran until 1953. Although not as popular as the Model A or Model B, it certainly held its place in Deere & Company's legacy.

WHERE'S F?

By 1937, the Letter Series John Deere tractors included Model A, Model B, Model C, and Model D tractors. The company used E for its stationary engines. Then IHC raced ahead with the Farmall F. Not wanting to confuse customers, Deere & Company skipped to Model G, as on this 1938 tractor. However, some parts already in production for Model Gs used the F code.

The space between the top radiator tank top and the steering shaft helps identify this as a low-radiator Model G that missed the company recall. About 3,200 copies like this were produced before engineers recalled them to fix the radiator and cooling system's overheating problem.

ೲ Letter Decoder ೦ೕ

Just like the GP tractor line, the Model A and Model B lines included many specialty versions. In fact, all John Deere tractor lines had variations on their themes. For example, the Model A theme included the AN, AW, AO, AOS, AR, ANH, AWH, AI, and AH.

N	One front wheel	R	Row-Crop: usually standard-tread; originally called AS	I	Industrial
W	Wide front axle			H	High-crop with extra clearance on both axles
O	Orchard design: low profile and side exhaust	NH	One front wheel, High-clearance rear axle	X	Experimental or prototype
OS	Orchard Streamlined design: shorter wheel-base for tighter turns	WH	Wide front axle, High-clearance rear axle	XO	Cross-over, also typically experimental

The 1937 Model 62 replaced the Model Y, but only 78 copies were produced.

DECISION NO. 7,900

In 1937, the Waterloo facility began work on its own small experimental tractor dubbed the Model H. The Deere & Company Decision No. 7,900, dated September 29, 1938, defined the role of the new tractor:

To meet the needs of small farms for limited power at low cost and for supplemental power on large farms, we will authorize the production of a lighter General Purpose Tractor designated as the Model H.

Introduced in 1939, the all-fuel Model H balanced record-setting mileage with decent but limited power for a wide range of uses. All Model Hs came styled and sported rubber tires. The low price and low-cost operation made Model Hs affordable for the four million small farmers who farmed 80 acres or less. More than 58,591 of them purchased a Model H.

This is a very early 1939 Model H.

JOHN DEERE

GROWING FOR VICTORY

RAIN FINALLY FELL ON THE PLAINS.

Farmers—at least, those who still owned farms—were happy to sweep the Dirty Thirties into the history books. The American economy flexed its muscles and Deere & Company shared the nation's growing strength.

In 1940, the company offered a solid line of tractors. The big tractors included the Model D and Model G. The Model A, Model B, and Model H offered mid-line power. The Model L and Model H covered the small end. Farmers everywhere could find just the right size John Deere tractor. And the lights still blazed in the R&D offices, promising a decade of even better things to come.

❧❧ Telltale Signs ❧❧

Lined up side by side, Model G is the largest, then A, then B, then H. But it's not so easy to know which is which when there's only one. Of course, the serial number plate is the best clue—but it's not always visible or attached.

MODEL G ❧

INTAKE STACK & **EXHAUST STACK** (always on driver's right)
    Unstyled: Stacks side by side
    Styled: Same

STEERING POST
    Smooth in the front; unbolts from the back

GRILL (styled models only)
    8 horizontal slots

MODEL A ❧

INTAKE STACK & **EXHAUST STACK**
    Unstyled: Stacks side by side
    Styled: Stacks aligned down tractor center;
        intake behind exhaust

STEERING POST
    Smooth in the front; unbolts from the back

GRILL (styled models only)
    8 horizontal slots

MODEL B ❧

INTAKE STACK & **EXHAUST STACK**
    Unstyled: Stacks side by side
    Styled: Stacks aligned down tractor center;
        intake behind exhaust

STEERING POST
    Removable plate on the front; 4 bolts

GRILL (styled models only)
    7 horizontal slots

MODEL H ❧

INTAKE STACK & **EXHAUST STACK**
    All styled: ONLY an exhaust stack; rectangular
    screen on the left side of the hood before "John"

STEERING POST
    Removable plate on the front; 2 bolts

GRILL (styled models only)
    7 slots

Running On Steel

During the war years, rubber supplies often ran short. Deere & Company shipped tractors such as the Model B and Model GM, like this 1942 version, on steel wheels. The two extra top-end gears were removed from the transmission to lower the speed for steel. Many owners missed the speed and added these two extra gears later when rubber tires were available.

Europe's second war, begun in 1939, rumbled in the distance. American farmers geared up to feed the battle-weary nations across the Atlantic Ocean. Then, on December 7, 1941, the Japanese attacked Pearl Harbor and America suddenly entered World War II. Everything changed.

As in the first World War, farmers joined the military. Wives and children stayed behind and worked the fields. They opted for easy-to-use equipment.

Farmers weren't the only folks joining the war effort. Deere & Co. employees, dealers, and their employees formed the U.S. Army 2nd Battalion, 3rd Ordnance Regiment in 1942. The John Deere Battalion served in Europe.

Starting in 1942, families dealt with food rationing and limits on sugar, gasoline, and other basics. The government set price controls and limited farm equipment, repair parts, and exports.

War restrictions blanked tractor production over and over, especially in late 1942 and early 1943. The company never managed to crank out more than 46 Model ANH vehicles in any war year. To stay busy, Deere & Company built MG-1 Military Tractors (bulldozers), ammunition, aircraft parts, and cargo and mobile laundry units.

1942 Model GM

H IS FOR HURTING

The firm stopped making the Model H series several times during World War II, halting production as long as 12 months. The war dented an already hurting Model H program.

Deere & Company had invested over $1 million to develop the Model H and introduced it in 1939—the same year that Henry Ford and Harry Ferguson unveiled their revolutionary Ford 9N with the Ferguson hydraulic system and three-point hitch, electric lights, electric start, and low cost. The new Ford-Ferguson 9N and 2N racked up sales of almost 200,000 units by the end of the war in 1945.

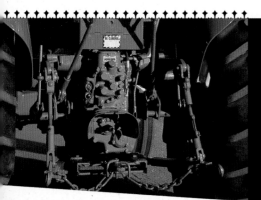

Easy Up And Down

The John Deere Model GP introduced the industry's first mechanical power lift in 1928—well ahead of the Ford 9N. But the Ford 9N Ferguson hydraulic lift system with its three-point hitch stole the show.

M NIPS AT N

Fortunately, Deere & Company already had a competition-ready tractor on the drawing board. Deere & Company introduced the Model M General Purpose Utility tractor in 1946. Its smallest tractor, the Model M replaced both the L and LA and took on Ford-Ferguson Model N tractors.

The Moline Tractor Works facility in Moline, Illinois developed the design. The company plant in Dubuque, Iowa actually built the Model M.

The Model M barely nipped at the N market.

This 1948 Model M and Quik-Tatch loader beat using a pitchfork to move a mountain of manure.

This 1950 Model M has one more horse than the Ford 9N. Still, the Ford 9N out-sold the Ms.

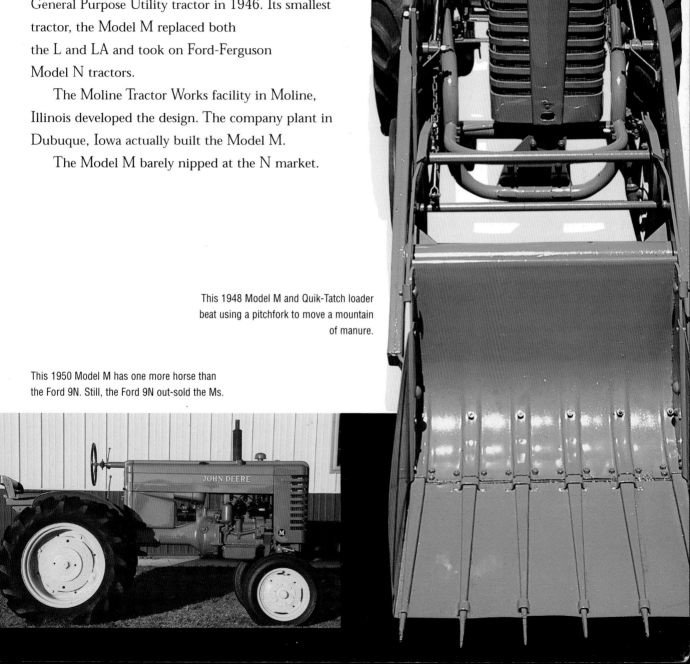

Style came to the farm aboard the 1939 John Deere Model A and Model B tractors, soon followed by the Model D. The slanted dash on this 1940 Model B made the gauges easy for the operator to read.

Tractor Style

For years, Deere & Company sold unstyled tractors. These skeleton-type vehicles had a simple hood for the fuel tank and no extra sheetmetal parts to hide the radiator.

In 1937, Deere & Company signed on with Henry Dreyfuss, a New York industrial designer gaining a worldwide reputation for making "pretty" practical. He gave the John Deere tractors a "family" look—each model line shared corporate characteristics.

Styled tractors featured a shaped hood that blended into the radiator cover. Sometimes called tinwork, styled parts such as fenders and dust shields added a finishing touch; they also kept the operator's platform much cleaner. Grouped instrument panels looked nice; they also made reading gauges and

reaching controls much easier. Dreyfuss and his team watched how farmers actually worked. So while their "corrugated" radiator shield or grill neatly dressed up a tractor, a farmer could clean it with gloved hands.

Dreyfuss engineers saw that farmers rode in the metal pan seat on their tractors for countless hours. In the mid-1940s, one of Dreyfuss' greatest successes for John Deere was a versatile cushioned seat and backrest.

In the 1950s, Dreyfuss blended this anthropometrics (the study of human dimensions and capabilities) with design, and applied it to all of Deere & Company's existing lines.

Henry Dreyfuss (1904–1972) profoundly changed the way American industry designed and presented its products.

Elephant Ears

Oversized or elongated clam-shell fenders, sometimes called elephant ears, kept the platform cleaner and operators happier.

POUR ON THE GAS

The peacetime economy put the war's technology to new uses. Agriculture leaped ahead with the innovations. Deere & Company introduced its advanced Powr-Trol hydraulic system in 1945.

Petroleum technology also advanced during and after World War II. Refineries focused on gasoline. Heavy fuel prices rose. Deere & Company switched to gasoline options, which also yielded more horsepower per unit of fuel than the heavy fuels.

DIESEL R-R-R-REVS UP

Rudolph D. Diesel perfected the diesel engine in 1892. Caterpillar began using this new power source in its crawlers in 1931. Two years later, International Harvester designed the first commercially successful diesel-powered wheel tractor. Deere & Company's diesel experiments started in the 1930s, too, and petered out.

Serious catch-up efforts started in the 1940s when Deere & Company engineers tackled the diesel start-up problem.

Because heavy diesel fuel needs high compression, mere mortals couldn't turn the flywheel. The R&D team built a gasoline-starting engine, nicknamed a pony engine, that could do it instead.

The Model R Diesel ran tough field tests before the production line cranked up in 1948. On rubber tires, it clocked forward speeds of approximately 2.12 to 11.5 miles per hour.

Regular production of the Model D ended in March 1953; but the 7,600-pound Model R slipped into its place before then.

No Spark In That Diesel?

Diesel fuel, sometimes called No. 2 fuel oil or distillate, doesn't vaporize and burn easily like gasoline does. So, an injection pump forces exactly the right amount of diesel fuel into the cylinder at exactly the right time. The high injection pressure and cylinder compression create heat to ignite the diesel fuel. Unlike gasoline engines, diesel engines don't use spark plugs or carburetors.

CHANGING WITH AMERICA

AS THE POSTWAR BOOM GAINED MOMENTUM, **THE NATION'S TRACTOR COUNT ROSE FROM APPROXIMATELY 2,000 IN 1910 TO 3,609,281 IN 1950.**

By 1950, most farmers had retired their horses and mules. The number of American farms was declining. With fewer but more demanding potential tractor customers, the industry sold fewer units. It would never again see a single model hit production numbers in the hundreds of thousands.

In 1953, after years of debate, Deere & Company decided to replace the beloved two-cylinder engine. The leaders opted for new four- and six-cylinder powerplants in an entirely new line that would bring together all the best engineering advances. Top-secret R&D for the "New Generation of Power" began.

The managers worried that any hard evidence that the two-cylinder tractors were being discontinued would kill sales and destroy the company. They insisted that the two-cylinder tractor line stay competitive and profitable until the New Generation multi-cylinders rolled out.

Deere & Company engineers had much more than New Generation tractors on their drawing boards. During the 1950s, the company introduced *three* new series of tractors: the first Numbered Series, the 20 Series, and the 30 Series. These lines would shoulder the load until the New Generation arrived.

An original 1952 Model A tractor pairs up with an early 1940s Model 12A combine.

Knee Highs

A true Hi-Crop vehicle had 33 inches of clearance under the rear axle. Longer spindles, sometimes called knees, allowed the extra clearance on the front axle. This 1952 Model G Hi-Crop is one of only 235 manufactured by Deere & Company.

THE FIRST NUMBERS

In 1952, Deere & Company's first Numbered Series tractors moved into production. They offered more horsepower and raised the bar for operator comfort and convenience.

Deere viewed the series as totally new tractors. Long lists of truly new features and handy options successfully blurred the shadow of the older Letter Series lurking under new tinwork.

MODEL 40 (REPLACED MODEL M)

The Model 40 Series featured a new hydraulic system with an industry-standard three-point hitch (*if you can't beat 'em, join 'em*!). Load-and-Depth Control regulated the working depth of mounted equipment to check that the planting depth or cultivating depth remained steady on uneven terrain or in varying soil conditions.

Farmers could select from 23 specially designed, rear-mounted three-point implements and four mid-mounted tools for the Model 40 Series. The other models in the series featured similar upgrades and options.

This 1955 Model 40V, Model 40 Special, or Model 40 Hi-Clearance came from the plant in Dubuque, Iowa.

On Model 40s and 50s, Cyclonic Fuel Intake used a cast arch, or eyebrow, over the intake valve on each cylinder to improve the air and fuel mixing. A better mixture meant better combustion within the cylinder, and that delivered more power.

MODEL 50 (REPLACED MODEL B)

The Model 50s after 1953 featured Duplex carburetion and Cyclonic Fuel Intake to boost the former Model B horsepower. Duplex carburetion was a single carburetor with two barrels. It supplied identical fuel mixture amounts to each cylinder.

MODEL 60 (REPLACED MODEL A)

The first Numbered Series tractor to be introduced in 1952, the Model 60 averaged 15,276 yearly units and nearly matched the extremely popular Model A yearly average of 16,600.

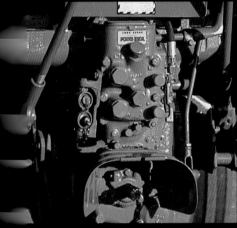

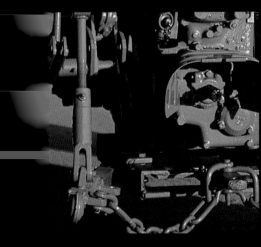

A Model 70's 376-cubic-inch, two-cylinder diesel puts the horses right here—45 on the drawbar and 50 on the belt pulley/PTO.

JOHN DEERE

MODEL 70 (REPLACED MODEL G)

The Model 70 offered a significant horsepower boost over the Model G. A diesel engine became available in 1954, making it the first John Deere diesel-powered row-crop tractor.

The full-instrument dash added style and convenience to this 1956 Model 80 Diesel.

MODEL 80 (REPLACED MODEL R)

Equipped with a standard front axle and a diesel engine, the Model 80 was the last of the first Numbered Series to be introduced. This diesel unit became the line's most powerful tractor.

Code Letters For Numbers

The Number Series introduced a new code for the model versions.

S = Standard
U = Utility
T = Tricycle
W = Row-Crop Utility

H = Hi-Crop
V = Special
C = Crawler
I = Industrial Specialty Utility

This 1956 Model 80 diesel, one of only 220 built without power steering, has a monster steering wheel.

JOHN DEERE DIESEL

80

BIGGER AND BETTER NUMBERS

When Deere & Company President Charles Deere Wiman died on May 12, 1955, William Hewitt, Wiman's son-in-law, became the sixth president of Deere & Company. Hewitt sought International Harvester Company's top spot in the agricultural machinery industry.

John Deere 20 and 30 Series tractors played an in convincing customers that the two-cylinder was improving, not disappearing.

The Dubuque-built 420 Series introduced in November 1955. The aggressive schedule pumped out the Waterloo-built 520, 620, 720, and 820 Models in August 1956, along with the Dubuque-built Model 320 Series.

This slant-steer 1957 Model 420 shows the new styling for 20 Series tractors.

Improvements in the piston, cylinder head, and ignition system added horsepower. They came in fewer versions, but offered plenty of options, such as gasoline or all-fuel engines and steel wheels for some models.

Deere & Company offered matching implements to handle any farming operation. The list for just the 420 included at least three dozen implements and attachments, from plows to planters, from peanut pullers to cotton pickers, and from corn shellers to cultivators.

This vibrant new look helped convince customers, and the competition, that Deere was committed to the two-cylinder tradition.

John Deere Family Lines

	LETTER SERIES	FIRST NUMBER SERIES	20 NUMBER SERIES	30 NUMBER SERIES	OTHER FAMILIES
M Family No.1	Model M		Model 320	Model 330	
M Family No.2	Model M	Model 40	Model 420	Model 430	Model 435 GM Diesel
B Family	Model B	Model 50	Model 520	Model 530	
A Family	Model A	Model 60	Model 620	Model 630	
G Family	Model G	Model 70	Model 720	Model 730	
Waterloo Boy Family	Model D and Model R Diesel	Model 80 Diesel	Model 820 Diesel	Model 830 Diesel	Model 840 Industrial Diesel

This 1960 Model 830 Rice Special offered more comfort and convenience with its facelift. The slanted steering wheel placed the gauges in an easy-to-read position.

This 1960 Model 430T Row-Crop unit with the tricycle front had the new 30 Series styling.

THE FINAL JOHNNY POPPER NUMBERS

Back in the late 1950s, Deere & Company's competition called the 30 Series tractors obsolete. Today, many people think these final two-cylinders were brilliant. The new Dreyfuss look included a more rounded hood line, a slanted dash and steering wheel, and a slightly different yellow hood stripe. The model-number typeface style changed and moved from low to high on the side of the radiator cowl.

Underneath the dressing, the 30 Series tractors were mechanically identical to their 20 Series parents. Deere & Company hoped new appearance, comfort, and convenience features would soothe customer doubts about the trusty two-cylinder's future.

Decisions, Decisions

Buying a John Deere 30 Series tractor meant making some serious decisions. Some of the choices:

- Speed-hour meter
- Fuel gauge
- Cigarette lighter
- Air stack and pre-cleaner
- Clam-shell fender
- Styled flat-topped fender with lights
- Weather brakes
- Float-Ride seat
- Rear muffler
- Custom Powr-Trol
- Single or dual remote hydraulic cylinder equipment
- Universal three-point hitch
- Load-and-Depth control
- Live PTO
- Front-frame, front-wheel, and rear-wheel weights

The Industrial Division also offered some models in industrial yellow, John Deere yellow, agricultural green and yellow, or any color the customer wanted—for a fee. The Industrial versions usually came with a heavy-duty front- and rear-axle package.

This 1960 Model 730 Diesel has many of the top options.

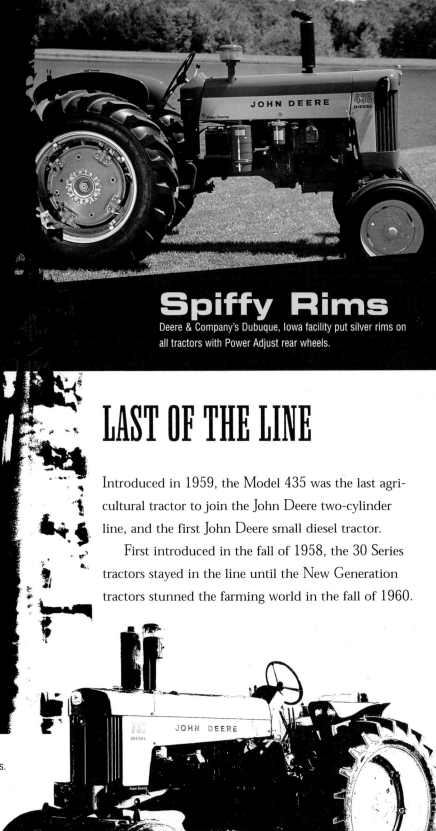

Spiffy Rims

Deere & Company's Dubuque, Iowa facility put silver rims on all tractors with Power Adjust rear wheels.

LAST OF THE LINE

Introduced in 1959, the Model 435 was the last agricultural tractor to join the John Deere two-cylinder line, and the first John Deere small diesel tractor.

First introduced in the fall of 1958, the 30 Series tractors stayed in the line until the New Generation tractors stunned the farming world in the fall of 1960.

CHAPTER FIVE TODAY

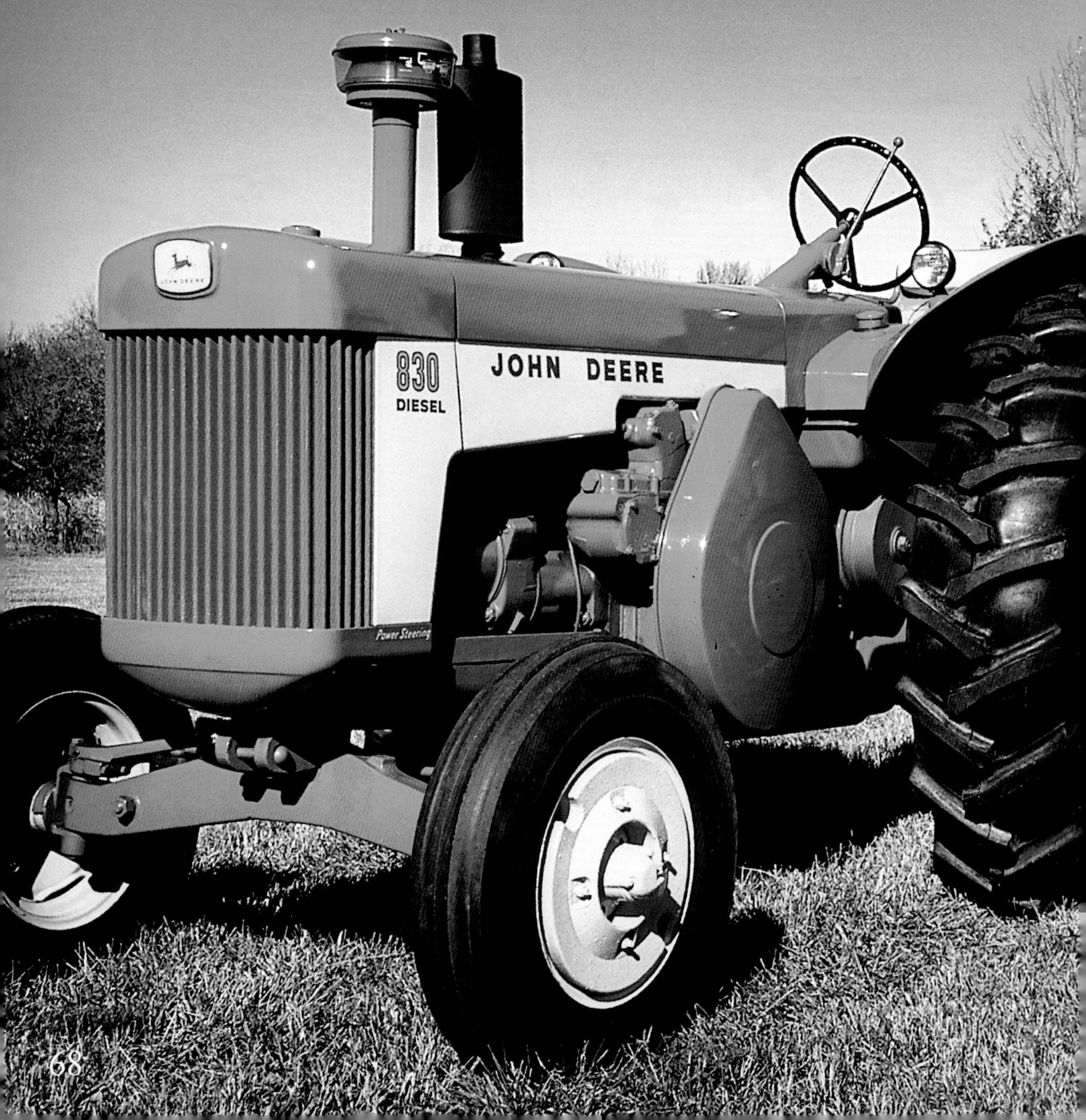

CELEBRATING THE LEGACY

THE TWO-CYLINDERS CARRIED THE LOAD FOR DEERE & COMPANY TRACTOR PROGRAM FOR JUST OVER FOUR DECADES.

A s planned, the new look of the 30 Series convinced the majority of dealers, farmers, and competitors that the two-cylinder was going to be around for many more years. They were right, because today, John Deere 30 Series and all Johnny Popper tractors are some of the most sought-after tractors on the planet.

THE WORLD LEADER

Deere & Company successfully introduced the New Generation tractors and swept into the top spot as the world's largest producer and seller of farm and industrial tractors and equipment by 1963.

In the years since then, the company has continued to advance agricultural machinery and set new benchmarks for the industry.

The company honors its two-cylinder heritage even today. The Deere & Company World Headquarters, which opened in 1964 in Moline, includes a display area for new and antique tractors and equipment. The facility also showcases a three-dimensional mural by Alexander Girard. Its 2,200 pieces of memorabilia span the company's first 75 years (1837–1918).

John Deere introduced the first commercially available rollover protective cages for farm tractors in 1966. Today, guards and shields help reduce tractor-related injuries and deaths. All tractor operators, especially drivers on tractors older than 1966, should always put safety first.

Award-Winning Design

Over the years, John Deere tractors have earned many awards. Even the Deere & Company World Headquarters earned international acclaim. Eero Saarinen, the same architect who created the Gateway Arch in St. Louis, Missouri, drew the plans but died just days before the project officially began. The headquarters opened in April 1964.

JOHN DEERE

Leaping Ahead

Deere & Company has used eight different John Deere logos since 1876. A new logo introduced in 2000 shows a leaping deer pushing upward rather than heading into a landing. It's the first time ever that the rear legs have touched the base.

RESTORING STORIES

Nostalgia drives many people to restore vintage John Deere tractors. Even non-farmers adore the old Johnny Poppers.

> "Now, when your dad was young—maybe about your age, he drove Grandpa Hank's old John Deere like a pro. The '46 had a hand clutch, see, that he could reach while he was backing up—made it easier for him to drive."

> "A Model D steel-wheeler held a straight line in the furrow and it pretty much drove itself. Sometimes, it did drive itself. Your Uncle Martin tied that John Deere in low gear and away she went, while he sat at one end of the field and ate his lunch. His fieldhand waited at the other end. When the tractor reached the end of the furrow, the fieldhand jumped on and turned it around. Then he hopped off and finished his lunch. Of course, the tractor got away from them from time to time! No, no, no, your Auntie didn't know! Of course, you could never do that with any other tractor then and you wouldn't do it with today's faster tractors—it's not safe."

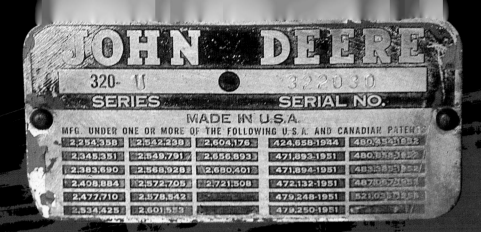

Restoration preserves the tractors. It also nurtures family stories, even the "secret" ones. Maybe that's part of the reason antique tractor restoration, activities, and clubs have grown remarkably since the turn into the twenty-first century.

Busy vintage tractor flea markets or swap meets usually feature junk tractors for donor parts as well as potential restoration projects. Sometimes restored models are for sale, too.

Collectors seek out certain models, often for sentimental reasons. They don't care if their favorite tractors were common or not.

People who collect Johnny Poppers for investment reasons usually shy away from the common tractors and hunt for tractors with low production numbers.

Serial Number Clues

Since the early days, every John Deere tractor receives a unique serial number plate that records the model and its production number. It provides clues about its past and its collector value. A very low number may mean a new model, while a very high number may mean it was the last of its kind.

For all research, an original source usually provides the most accurate details. The John Deere Collectors Center opened in 2001 in Moline and specializes in pre-1960 two-cylinder tractors. Actual restoration work in progress, vintage tractor displays, a store, consignment opportunities, and a customer service counter with reference materials and old parts information attract visitors from around the world.

Restoration projects need a work area, tools, mechanical skills, painting skills, and some general fabrication knowledge. Certain jobs, such as diesel fuel injector repairs, require a professional mechanic. Each project consumes loads of patience (and time), and usually a serious chunk of change—probably nothing less than $5,000 for a basic restoration job.

All restoration requires research. In addition to checking the serial number, restorers want to learn the vehicle's history. Where did it operate? What did it do? Where was it stored and how well was it maintained?

Restorers also try to determine what original parts and options were on the vehicle. Original parts books, dealer brochures, restoration books and magazines, and online restoration sites offer clues.

Then restorers spend countless hours searching for just the right components. It's a treasure hunt for grown-ups. Often, restorers build one vehicle using parts and pieces rescued from several "donors." Johnny Popper clubs, Web sites, and the folks at Deere & Company can help. And nothing beats listening to a farmer who spent countless hours onboard a Johnny Popper—he or she usually knows loads of details.

Every collector dreams about that one crown in the collection. Sometimes it's rare, like this Model 620 LP-gas tractor. It's one of only 37 ever manufactured. Sometimes it's the one Grandpa drove. The list below includes tractors that aren't all that old, but low production numbers make them collector treasures.

1930 GP X/O	Production: 68
1941–1945 Model HNH	Production: 37
Model 620 LP-gas	Production: 37
Model 620 Hi-Crop LP-gas	Production: 48
Model 630 Hi-Crop LP-gas	Production: 3 (plus 5 all-fuel and 11 gasoline)
Model 720 Hi-Crop	Production: 125
Model 730 Hi-Crop	Production: 123
Model 430 Standard LP-gas	Production: 5 (plus 18 all-fuel and 1,786 gasoline)
Model 430 Hi-Crop LP-gas	Production: 5

RESTORATION CELEBRATIONS

Proud owners of restored Johnny Poppers love to show off the results. They ride in parades, local fairs, and community events. They also gather at the hundreds of vintage tractor shows and "meets" across the United States, Canada, and Europe held every year. Some events focus on certain brands, such as the "Reunion on the River" in Moline for John Deere enthusiasts. Other shows invite any and all steam- and gasoline-powered models.

"Slow races" at vintage tractor shows test the drivers' ability to cover a certain distance in the slowest time without stalling the engine.

Antique tractor pulls have gained popularity in recent years. They deliver all the excitement of modern tractor pulls, but without the hype and expense. Most vintage tractors in these events look much like the original, but with extra weight racks and wheelie bars. Many work around the farm or acreage when they're not competing.

MUSEUMS OF THE RESTORATION ARTS

Some people say that restoration is an art. Many American museums display restored vintage tractors:

- The Lester F. Larsen Tractor Test & Power Museum in Lincoln, Nebraska
- The Smithsonian in Washington, D.C.
- The John Deere Pavilion in Moline, Illinois
- Several working history farm museums across the U.S.

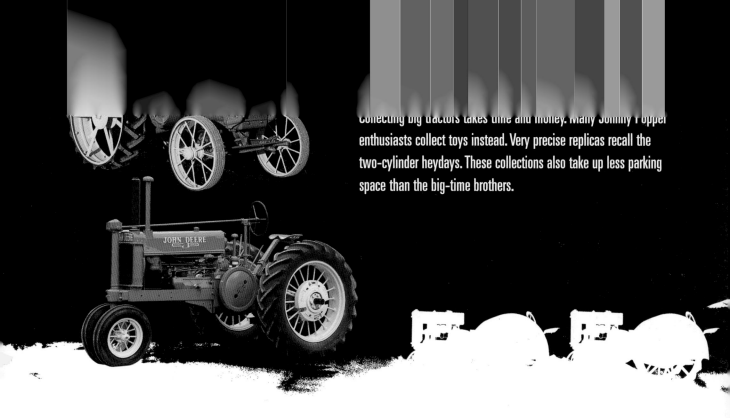

Collecting big tractors takes time and money. Many Johnny Popper enthusiasts collect toys instead. Very precise replicas recall the two-cylinder heydays. These collections also take up less parking space than the big-time brothers.

John Deere tractors are an authentic part of the American experience from coast to coast. For many people, these machines symbolize a link to the family farm and a proud rural heritage. The unique Johnny Popper sound carries stories across generations and holds a special place in history.

JUST LISTEN.

JOHN DEERE TIMELINE

1837: John Deere creates a polished-steel plow.

1841: The first practical grain drill is patented.

1848: John Deere moves his growing plow business to Moline, Illinois.

1849: The John Deere company builds 2,136 plows.

1853: Charles Deere joins the company as a bookkeeper.

1859: Charles Deere takes over the business.

1863: The Hawkeye Riding Cultivator is manufactured, the first John Deere implement that allows for riding.

1875: The Gilpin Sulky Plow is created by Gilpin Moore and turns out to be one of John Deere's most successful products of the nineteenth century.

1876: The "leaping deer" trademark appears.

1880: Wagons enter the product line, soon followed by buggies.

1886: John Deere dies at age 82 in Moline, Illinois.

1894: As bicycles gain popularity, the Deere Leader, Deere Roadster, and Moline Special are advertised in catalogs.

1907: Charles Deere dies, succeeded by son-in-law William Butterworth.

1912: Deere & Company is made up of 11 manufacturing entities in the United States, and 1 in Canada.

1918: Waterloo Boy tractor manufacturer is purchased by Deere.

1923: The Model D premiers.

1929: Deere introduces the GP Wide-Tread.

1934: Deere introduces the Model A.

1935: Deere follows up with the Model B.

1939: Model L tractors get a restyling from Henry Dreyfuss.

1943: Deere manufactures military tractors and other supplies during World War II.

1947: The Model M is manufactured at Dubuque Works.

1949: The Model R debuts, Deere's first diesel-powered tractor.

1953: Deere premiers the largest row-crop tractor to date: the Model 70.

1955: After the passing of Charles Deere Wiman, William A. Hewitt is elected president.

1957: John Deere introduces six-row planters and cultivators.

1959: The 215-horsepower 8010 debuts, powered by a diesel motor.

1963: John Deere becomes the world's largest producer and seller of farm/industrial equipment.

1966: Total sales exceed $1 billion.

1968: Lawn and garden tractors are offered with optional color schemes.

1971: Deere advertises snowmobiles, with the slogan "Nothing runs like a Deere."

1980: The industry's first four-row cotton picker is premiered by Deere.

1982: Chairman William A. Hewitt retires, succeeded by Robert A. Hanson.

1987: The 150th anniversary is celebrated.

1990: Hans W. Becherer succeeds Robert Hanson as Chairman.

1996: Deere introduces four mid-priced lawn tractors and two walk-behind mowers branded "Sabre by John Deere."

1997: Overseas sales exceed $3 billion.

2000: Robert W. Lane is elected CEO after Hans Becherer retires.

2005: A seeding-equipment assembly plant is opened in Orenburg, Russia.

GLOSSARY

agriculture (AG ri kul cher) work or study concerned with land, crops, livestock or poultry; farming

bore (BOHR) in an engine, the hollowed area inside a cylinder for the piston; John Deere two-cylinder tractors have used many different bore sizes over the years

belt pulley (BELT PUL ee) a device on a tractor that runs other farm equipment

carburetor (KAR bah ray tur) a device for mixing fuel with air for the engine to burn

chassis (CHASS ee) the frame that supports the body of a vehicle

clutch (KLUCH) in an engine, a mechanical device for engaging or disengaging a shaft with or from another shaft or spinning part

compression (kom PRESH en) in an engine's cylinder, the result of a piston stroke toward the cylinder top that reduces volume and increases pressure on the air and fuel mix

crankshaft (KRANGK shaft) in an engine, the shaft attached to the piston; the pistons turn the crankshaft

cultivator (KUL tah VAY tur) a tool drawn between rows of growing plants to loosen the earth and destroy weeds

Cyclonic Fuel Intake (SIH klon ik FYOO el IN tayk) the John Deere name for a cast arch, or eyebrow, over the intake valve on each cylinder to improve the air and fuel mixing

cylinder (SIL in dur) in an engine, a rounded and hollowed chamber fitted with a sliding piston; in John Deere two-cylinder tractors, the cylinders were positioned opposite of each other or vertically, depending on the model and year

Duplex carburetion (DOO pleks KAR bah ray shun) the John Deere name for a single carburetor system with two barrels supplying identical fuel mixture amounts to each cylinder

drawbar (DRAH bar) the heavy bar at the rear of a tractor used as a hitch to pull machinery, such as a plow

drawbar horsepower (DRAH bar HORS pow ur) the measure of the final horsepower sent to the drawbar to pull an implement; always less than the indicated horsepower

flywheel (flih WEEL) a heavy disk or wheel that spins a shaft and the parts connected to the shaft

full-line manufacturer (FUL lihn MAN yoo FAK chur ur) a company that makes most or all of the related products used for a certain job or industry

horsepower (HORS pow ur) a unit of power equal to lifting 550 pounds to a one-foot height in one second or 33,000 pounds to a one-foot height in one minute

ignition (ig NISH un) in an engine, the process that sets the fuel on fire inside the cylinder; this fire is like a fast explosion

implement (IM pluh ment) a tool or device that performs a certain task

indicated horsepower (IN di KAYT ed HORS pow ur) an engine's highest horsepower rating, which reflects its cylinder pressure

memorabilia (MEM ur ah BIHL ee yah) things that recall an event or time period

nostalgia (nah STAL jee ah) pleasant memories or thoughts about a time in the past

overhead steering (OH vur HED STEER ing) on a John Deere tractor, the system that use a long steering shaft positioned above the main engine area

piston (PIS ten) a tightly fitting disk or cylinder-shaped device that moves back and forth inside the engine cylinder's bore or hollowed area; in a four-stroke engine common to pre-1960 John Deere tractors, the piston completes its cycle in four strokes:

- Stroke 1 - piston slides back and sucks in the air and fuel mix

- Stroke 2 – piston slides upward and builds pressure and ignites the fuel

- Stroke 3 – piston slides back due to the explosive force of ignition

- Stroke 4 – piston returns upward and pushes out the exhaust from the burned fuel

power take-off unit (POW ur TAYK ahff YOO nit) called the PTO, the metal pole at the rear of the tractor that carries power from the tractor's engine to an implement, which is usually hitched to the tractor at three metal links

replica (REP li kah) a copy of an original item

restoration (res tah RAY shun) the process of returning something to its original condition

stationary engine (STAY shu NER ee en JIN) an engine that stays in one place as it powers other equipment, tools, or accessories

transmission (trans MISH un) in vehicles, the unit of gears that allows the engine's power to move the wheels

tricycle front-end (TRIH si kul FRONT end) an early tractor design with two widely spaced large rear wheels and one front tire; designed to allow tractors to make very tight turns at the end of a furrow, the single wheel turned but "plowed" into the soil, so double-wheel tricycle front-ends became standard

two-lunger (too LUNG ur) a nickname for the two-cylinder engine design where air mixes with fuel; a one-lunger means an engine with one cylinder

Index